BEST MUG CAKES EVER

BEST
MUG
CAKES
EVER

TREAT YOURSELF TO HOMEMADE CAKE FOR ONE IN FIVE MINUTES OR LESS

monica sweeney

THE COUNTRYMAN PRESS · WOODSTOCK · VT.

Mug Cake Photo Credits

All Photos by Allan Penn unless otherwise indicated, below:

Page 9: © motorolka/veer.com; 11: © vetkit/veer.com; 16, 17, 23: © jirkaejc/veer.com; 27: © Igna Nielsen/veer.com; 25: © Volff/veer.com; 35: © karandaev/veer.com; 36: © Beth Swanson/veer.com; 38, 39: © Quanthem/veer.com; 46: © nowshika/veer.com; 54: © Ionescu Bogdan Cristian/veer.com; 57: © Chris Dorney/veer.com; 58, 59: © Eva Gruendemann/veer.com; 60: © marilyna/veer.com; 64, 93: © nowshika/veer.com; 67: © gunnar3000/veer.com; 71: © rgebbiephoto/veer.com; 72: © GooDween/veer.com; 76: © Serghei Platonov/veer.com; 79: © Kaarsten/veer.com; 80, 81: © luchschen/veer.com; 87, 90: © Alexstar/veer.com; 95: © Dolphy/dreamstime.com; 97, 100: © cristi180884/veer.com; 98, 99, 112: © charlotteLake/veer.com; 110: © Elenathewise/veer.com; 114: © ericro/veer.com; 116: © molka/veer.com; 117: © Brooke Photo Studio/veer.com;

Best Mug Cakes Ever

ISBN978-1-58157-273-5

Published by The Countryman Press, P.O. Box 748, Woodstock, VT 05091

Distributed by W. W. Norton & Company, Inc., 500 Fifth Avenue, New York, NY 10110

Printed in United States

10 9 8 7 6 5 4 3 2 1

TO HOLLY SCHMIDT AND ALLAN PENN,
FOR YOUR INSPIRING DEDICATION
TO BAKED GOODS.

BEST MUG CAKES EVER

CONTENTS

Chapter Four: Boozy Bites / 81

Chapter Five: Beyond Cakes / 99

Introduction: Mug Cake Basics

Mug cakes are a revolutionary discovery for people who crave homemade cake. It is almost unbelievable that you can mix a few simple ingredients together in a mug and—*presto*!—you are rewarded with a warm, delicious, homemade cake in less than 5 minutes from start to finish! But it's true, and in this book I will show you how easy it is to create 50 different kinds of mug cakes using ingredients you can keep on hand so you are prepared whenever the craving hits.

What Size Mug to Use?

Each of the recipes in this book is scaled to make one hearty portion. I have fairly large mugs, so if your mug is much smaller, you may need to adjust the proportions to make less batter, or save the extra for another cake. It is important that you never fill the mug more than halfway, or you are likely to end up with a messy cake explosion in your microwave when it bubbles over. You will probably figure out pretty quickly which of your mugs is best for this—it has to be microwave-safe (obviously) and the right size, and it helps if it isn't one of those mugs that gets burning hot in the microwave. You can also put the batter into a ramekin or microwave-safe bowl if you want, but it will be less cute that way.

The instructions for the cakes call for mixing everything right in the mug, which makes for an easy cleanup. However, you might find you prefer to mix the ingredients in a separate bowl or measuring cup and pour the batter into the mug, which makes for a cleaner presentation of the finished cake. It is entirely up to you.

Ingredients and Measuring

The ingredients in these recipes are mostly pantry staples that you can keep on hand, which is one of the magnificent benefits of mug cakes. There are two ingredients, however, that deserve special explanation.

SELF-RISING FLOUR

Self-rising flour, which is just flour with baking powder and salt added to it, is featured in almost every recipe in this book, and is readily available at any supermarket. It cuts down on the number of ingredients you need to pull out of your cabinets and measure to make each cake, so it's a real time-saver when you are making something as quick and easy as a mug cake. You can make your own self-rising flour if you don't have it on hand.

SELF-RISING FLOUR
1 cup all-purpose flour
1 1/2 teaspoons baking powder
1/4 teaspoon salt

Mix all ingredients together and store in an airtight container.

Eggs/Liquid Egg Substitute

One of the challenges in adapting standard cake recipes to mugs is how to address the egg issue. A regular layer cake has 2 or 3 eggs in 12 servings—for a single-serving cake, using a whole egg would make an overly eggy cake. After some experimentation, I determined that 2 tablespoons of beaten egg is the right amount for most mug cakes. You can achieve this a couple of different ways: You can beat an egg and measure out 2 tablespoons, then save the rest for another use, or you can use liquid egg substitute (like Egg Beaters). Egg Beaters are always good to have on hand, since they keep for a long time and are super easy to use.

Cooking Time

Unlike regular ovens, which are calibrated to standard temperatures, microwave ovens vary in strength. You will have to experiment with cooking times to determine the right one for your microwave. The first time you make a mug cake, stop the cooking and check it for doneness after about 45 seconds. If it is done, the sides will have pulled away from the mug and the top will look set, but not totally dry. If it's still runny in the middle, cook it at 15-second intervals until it is done. You don't want to overcook your mug cake, as it will become rubbery and dry.

The temperature of your ingredients will affect the cooking time, so plan to cook a mug cake longer if it has frozen or cold fruit or liquids in it. Some of the denser cakes (like Banana) take a little longer to cook.

After you try it a couple of times, you will know exactly how long your microwave takes to cook a mug cake and can adjust the recommended cooking times here accordingly.

Enjoy the sweet, simple cup of comfort that awaits you!

BEST MUG CAKES EVER

CHAPTER ONE

SWEET AND SIMPLE

Chocolate Brownie

The classic indulgence that kicked off the mug cake craze, this rich, chocolate treat is a thing of absolute beauty. You will never believe you can make such a decadent chocolate cake in just a few minutes!

4 tablespoons self-rising flour

4 tablespoons sugar

3 tablespoons cocoa powder

2 tablespoons beaten egg or liquid egg substitute

3 tablespoons milk

2 tablespoons vegetable oil

1/2 teaspoon vanilla extract

Mix the flour, sugar, and cocoa powder in a mug. Add the egg, milk, oil, and vanilla and stir until well combined. Microwave on high for 1 minute or until the top is just dry.

"First we eat, then we do everything else."

— M. F. K. Fisher

Classic Yellow

A delicious little birthday cake in a mug! This is great with a scoop of ice cream, or go the extra mile and whip up a simple frosting to smear on top. This cake has lots of rich vanilla flavor and a moist, tender texture that can easily stand alone, but is truly excellent topped with fresh berries.

4 tablespoons self-rising flour

4 tablespoons sugar

2 tablespoons beaten egg or liquid egg substitute

3 tablespoons milk

2 tablespoons vegetable oil

1/2 teaspoon vanilla extract

Mix the flour and sugar in a mug. Add the egg, milk, oil, and vanilla and stir until well combined. Microwave on high for 1 minute or until the top is just dry.

Espresso

A coffee lover's perfect little dessert, this cappuccino-flavored treat is also a great breakfast indulgence! Like flavored coffee? Throw in a little hazelnut, French vanilla, or other coffee flavoring with the liquid ingredients. No barista required.

4 tablespoons self-rising flour

4 tablespoons sugar

1 teaspoon instant espresso powder

2 tablespoons beaten egg or liquid egg substitute

3 tablespoons milk

2 tablespoons vegetable oil

1/2 teaspoon vanilla extract

Mix the flour, sugar, and espresso powder in a mug. Add the egg, milk, oil, and vanilla and stir until well combined. Microwave on high for 1 minute or until the top is just dry.

Red Velvet

Red velvet cake gets its characteristic color from a heavy dose of red food coloring, and most recipes only include a little bit of cocoa powder. I upped the cocoa powder significantly for mine to give it a stronger chocolate flavor, which I think tastes better. But if you want the classic rose-red color you see in bakery red velvet cake, reduce the cocoa powder to 1 tablespoon.

4 tablespoons self-rising flour

4 tablespoons sugar

3 tablespoons cocoa powder

2 tablespoons beaten egg or liquid egg substitute

1 tablespoon red food coloring

3 tablespoons vegetable oil

3 tablespoons buttermilk

Mix the flour, sugar, and cocoa powder in a mug. Add the egg, food coloring, oil, and buttermilk and stir until well combined. Microwave on high for 1 1/2 minutes or until the top is just dry. Frost with Cream Cheese Frosting.

CREAM CHEESE FROSTING

2 ounces cream cheese, softened

2 tablespoons unsalted butter, softened

1/2 teaspoon vanilla extract

1/2 cup powdered sugar

Beat the cream cheese and butter with an electric mixer until fluffy. Add the vanilla and powdered sugar and beat until smooth.

Vegan Coconut

The coconut milk in this easy mug cake takes the place of all the other liquids, including the eggs and milk, making this an easy vegan treat. Feel free to throw in some chocolate chips or a drizzle of chocolate sauce for a Mounds-like experience.

4 tablespoons self-rising flour

2 1/2 tablespoons sugar

4 tablespoons full-fat coconut milk

1/2 teaspoon vanilla extract

1 tablespoon sweetened shredded coconut

Mix the flour and sugar in a mug. Add the coconut milk and vanilla and mix until well combined. Stir in the coconut. Microwave on high for 1 minute or until the top is just dry.

Maple Walnut

Maple syrup takes the place of sugar in this sweet, nutty cake that is reminiscent of an old-fashioned ice cream flavor. It is delicious with a scoop of vanilla ice cream and also great on its own.

5 tablespoons self-rising flour

2 tablespoons pure maple syrup

2 tablespoons beaten egg or liquid egg substitute

1 tablespoon vegetable oil

1 1/2 tablespoons milk

1 tablespoon chopped walnuts

Put the flour in a mug. Add the maple syrup, egg, oil, and milk. Mix until well combined. Stir in the walnuts. Microwave on high for 1 minute or until the top is just dry.

"I am not a glutton. I am an explorer of food."

—Erma Bombeck

Peanut Butter and Fluff

If you have peanut butter cravings, this one is for you! The fluff is a perfect, ready-to-spread frosting for this simple cake, and will make this a favorite go-to treat.

4 tablespoons self-rising flour

4 tablespoons sugar

2 tablespoons beaten egg or liquid egg substitute

3 tablespoons peanut butter

3 tablespoons milk

1 tablespoon vegetable oil

2 tablespoons Marshmallow Fluff

Mix the flour and sugar in a mug. Add the egg, peanut butter, milk, and oil and mix well to combine. Microwave on high for 1 1/2 minutes or until the top is just dry. Top with Marshmallow Fluff.

Butterscotch Brownie

Dark brown sugar and butter combine in this decadent cake to make a rich butterscotch flavor. Studded with chocolate and butterscotch chips, this cake is the buttery, chocolaty stuff of dreams.

4 tablespoons self-rising flour

4 tablespoons dark brown sugar

2 tablespoons beaten egg or liquid egg substitute

3 tablespoons milk

1/2 teaspoon vanilla extract

3 tablespoons unsalted butter, melted

2 tablespoons semi-sweet chocolate chips, butterscotch chips, or a mix of both

Mix the flour and sugar in a mug. Add the egg, milk, vanilla, and melted butter and mix well to combine. Stir in the chips and microwave on high for 1 minute or until the top is just dry.

"'Tis an ill cook that cannot lick his own fingers."

—William Shakespeare

Candy Cane

A peppermint refresher with the sweet crunch of candy canes! This is great drizzled with chocolate sauce, and a perfect treat for the holidays or a cold, snowy afternoon.

4 tablespoons self-rising flour

4 tablespoons sugar

2 tablespoons beaten egg or liquid egg substitute

3 tablespoons milk

2 tablespoons vegetable oil

1/4 teaspoon peppermint extract

1 candy cane or 4 round peppermint hard candies, crushed

Mix the flour and sugar in a mug. Add the egg, milk, oil, and peppermint extract and mix well to combine. Stir in the crushed candy. Microwave on high for 1 minute or until the top is just dry.

Confetti

If you are a fan of birthday-cake-flavored treats, this is the mug cake for you. Shot through with colorful sprinkles, it's a delight to look at and even more wonderful to eat.

4 tablespoons self-rising flour

4 tablespoons sugar

2 tablespoons beaten egg or liquid egg substitute

3 tablespoons milk

2 tablespoons vegetable oil

1/2 teaspoon vanilla extract

2 tablespoons multicolored sprinkles

Mix the flour and sugar in a mug. Add the egg, milk, oil, and vanilla and stir until well combined. Stir in the sprinkles. Microwave on high for 1 minute or until the top is just dry.

"A party without cake is just a meeting."

—Julia Child

CHAPTER TWO

CHOCOLATE INDULGENCE

Chocolate Salted Caramel

Salted caramel is a ubiquitous flavor in many desserts and candied treats, and for good reason: The buttery, creamy caramel is perfectly complemented by the crunchy sea salt. And when swirled into a fudgy chocolate cake, it is divine. You can either use store-bought caramel sauce, or throw a few unwrapped caramel candies into a ramekin and microwave at 50 percent power for a minute or two to melt them.

4 tablespoons self-rising flour

4 tablespoons sugar

3 tablespoons cocoa powder

2 tablespoons beaten egg or liquid egg substitute

3 tablespoons milk

2 tablespoons vegetable oil

1/2 teaspoon vanilla extract

2 tablespoons caramel sauce or 1 ounce solid caramel, melted

Sea salt

Mix the flour, sugar, and cocoa powder in a mug. Add the egg, milk, oil, and vanilla and stir until well combined. Swirl in the caramel sauce or melted caramel and sprinkle the top with sea salt. Microwave on high for 1 minute or until the top is just dry.

"The secret of success in life is to eat what you like and let the food fight it out inside."

—Mark Twain

Chocolate Hazelnut

This one is all about the Nutella! This easy mug cake puts the addictive flavor combination of chocolate and hazelnut front and center. Instead of spreading it on apples or toast (or just eating it straight from the jar), test out the delicious chocolate-hazelnut flavor in this amazing little indulgence.

4 tablespoons self-rising flour

4 tablespoons sugar

3 tablespoons cocoa powder

2 tablespoons beaten egg or liquid egg substitute

3 tablespoons milk

2 tablespoons vegetable oil

3 tablespoons chocolate-hazelnut spread (like Nutella)

1/2 teaspoon vanilla extract

1 tablespoon chopped hazelnuts (optional)

Mix the flour, sugar, and cocoa powder in a mug. Add the egg, milk, oil, chocolate-hazelnut spread, and vanilla and stir until well combined. Top with the chopped hazelnuts, if using. Microwave on high for 1 minute or until the top is just dry.

"All you need is love. But a little chocolate now and then doesn't hurt."
—Charles M. Schulz

Chocolate Peanut Butter

Ahh, the classic combo! This mug cake has a hidden surprise—a nugget of peanut butter hidden in the middle of a dark chocolate cake! It's a peanut butter cup lover's dream. Try it with peanut butter chips or chocolate chips if you don't have the candy on hand.

4 tablespoons self-rising flour

4 tablespoons sugar

3 tablespoons cocoa powder

2 tablespoons beaten egg or liquid egg substitute

3 tablespoons milk

2 tablespoons vegetable oil

1/2 teaspoon vanilla extract

1 tablespoon peanut butter

2 heaping tablespoons chopped peanut butter cups or chocolate and/or peanut butter chips

Mix the flour, sugar, and cocoa powder in a mug. Add the egg, milk, oil, and vanilla and stir until well combined. With a spoon, make a well in the center of the batter and drop in the peanut butter, smoothing the cake batter back into place on top of it. Top with the chopped Reese's. Microwave on high for 1 minute or until the top is just dry.

S'More

The campfire favorite in a mug! This little mug cake swaps out the traditional chocolate bar for a rich chocolate cake, studded with graham crackers and topped with marshmallows. You have all the flavor of the original without the risk of a charred marshmallow.

4 tablespoons self-rising flour

4 tablespoons sugar

3 tablespoons cocoa powder

2 tablespoons beaten egg or liquid egg substitute

3 tablespoons milk

2 tablespoons vegetable oil

1/2 teaspoon vanilla extract

2 graham crackers, broken into pieces

Handful of miniature marshmallows

Mix the flour, sugar, and cocoa powder in a mug. Add the egg, milk, oil, and vanilla and stir until well combined. Shove the graham cracker pieces into the cake batter so that they're evenly distributed. Top the cake with miniature marshmallows. Microwave on high for 1 minute or until the top is just dry. For added texture, use a kitchen torch to crisp the marshmallow.

"I think every woman should have a blowtorch."
—Julia Child

Chocolate Cherry

A Black Forest cake in a mug, made super easy by the use of frozen pitted cherries, which you can find in any supermarket these days. If you happen to have some chocolate-covered cherries lying around, put one on top of the finished cake to turn a simple treat into a showstopper.

4 tablespoons self-rising flour

4 tablespoons sugar

3 tablespoons cocoa powder

2 tablespoons beaten egg or liquid egg substitute

3 tablespoons milk

2 tablespoons vegetable oil

1/2 teaspoon vanilla extract

1/4 cup fresh or frozen pitted dark sweet cherries, thawed if frozen

Mix the flour, sugar, and cocoa powder in a mug. Add the egg, milk, oil, and vanilla and stir until well combined. Fold in the cherries. Microwave on high for 1 1/2 to 2 minutes or until the top is just dry.

"He who distinguishes the true savor of his food can never be a glutton; he who does not cannot be otherwise."

—Henry David Thoreau

Grasshopper

If you are a fan of Girl Scout Thin Mints, you will swoon over this cake! A dark, fudgy chocolate cake with a hint of mint flavor, topped with crushed Andes candies, this dessert is a mint chocolate chip lover's delight.

4 tablespoons self-rising flour

4 tablespoons sugar

3 tablespoons cocoa powder

2 tablespoons beaten egg or liquid egg substitute

3 tablespoons milk

2 tablespoons vegetable oil

1/4 teaspoon peppermint extract

Handful of Andes candies bits, or three whole Andes candies, chopped

Mix the flour, sugar, and cocoa powder in a mug. Add the egg, milk, oil, and peppermint extract and stir until well combined. Top with Andes candies. Microwave on high for 1 minute or until the top is just dry.

"Let's face it, a nice creamy chocolate cake does a lot for a lot of people; it does for me."

—Audrey Hepburn

Bittersweet Mocha

A sophisticated, dark chocolate cake that is elegant enough for a dinner party, but easy enough to make as an after-dinner treat for yourself. You can adjust the amount of espresso powder to control the strength of the coffee flavor.

4 tablespoons self-rising flour

4 tablespoons sugar

3 tablespoons cocoa powder

1/2 teaspoon instant espresso powder

2 tablespoons beaten egg or liquid egg substitute

3 tablespoons milk

2 tablespoons vegetable oil

1/2 teaspoon vanilla extract

1/4 cup bittersweet chocolate chips

Mix the flour, sugar, cocoa powder, and espresso powder in a mug. Add the egg, milk, oil, and vanilla and stir until well combined. Stir in the chocolate chips. Microwave on high for 1 minute or until the top is just dry.

"Never eat more than you can lift."

—Miss Piggy

Chocolate Raspberry

A dark chocolate cake bursting with the taste of fresh raspberries, this is surprisingly easy to put together. The addition of a layer of raspberry jam brings an extra boost of raspberry flavor—top with a fresh raspberry or two and you have an elegant dessert that tastes like it took all day!

4 tablespoons self-rising flour

5 tablespoons sugar

3 tablespoons cocoa powder

2 tablespoons beaten egg or liquid egg substitute

3 tablespoons milk

2 tablespoons vegetable oil

1/2 teaspoon vanilla extract

1/4 cup frozen raspberries, thawed

2 tablespoons seedless raspberry jam

Mix the flour, sugar, and cocoa powder in a mug. Add the egg, milk, oil, and vanilla and stir until well combined. Fold in the raspberries. Spread the raspberry jam on top. Microwave on high for 1 1/2 to 2 minutes or until the top is just dry.

"I'm pretty sure that eating chocolate keeps wrinkles away because I have never seen a ten-year-old with a Hershey bar and crow's-feet."

—Amy Neftzger

Chocolate-Covered Pretzel

The salty-sweet combination of chocolate-covered pretzels meets the comfort of cake. The contrasting crunch they give to the soft cake makes for a texturally interesting treat that will have you craving more!

    4 tablespoons self-rising flour

    4 tablespoons sugar

    3 tablespoons cocoa powder

    2 tablespoons beaten egg or liquid egg substitute

    3 tablespoons milk

    2 tablespoons vegetable oil

    1/2 teaspoon vanilla extract

    5 small chocolate-covered pretzels, broken into pieces

Mix the flour, sugar, and cocoa powder in a mug. Add the egg, milk, oil, and vanilla and stir until well combined. Fold in the chocolate-covered pretzels. Microwave on high for 1 minute or until the top is just dry.

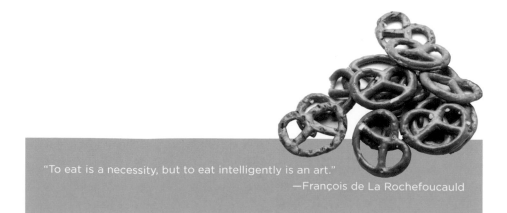

"To eat is a necessity, but to eat intelligently is an art."
—François de La Rochefoucauld

Cookies and Cream

For die-hard chocoholics, this cake is flawless with chocolate batter. But if you prefer that classic cookies 'n' cream flavor, you can make this with the Classic Yellow Mug Cake recipe (page 20) instead.

- 4 tablespoons self-rising flour
- 4 tablespoons sugar
- 3 tablespoons cocoa powder
- 2 tablespoons beaten egg or liquid egg substitute
- 3 tablespoons milk
- 2 tablespoons vegetable oil
- 1/2 teaspoon vanilla extract
- 3 chocolate sandwich cookies, crushed into coarse crumbs, divided

Mix the flour, sugar, and cocoa powder in a mug. Add the egg, milk, oil, and vanilla and stir until well combined. Fold in two-thirds of the cookie crumbs and top with the remaining crumbs. Microwave on high for 1 minute or until the top is just dry.

"Health food may be good for the conscience but Oreos taste a hell of a lot better."

—Robert Redford

CHAPTER THREE

FRUITY SWEETS

Strawberry Vanilla

An easy vanilla cake with a sweet swirl of strawberry jam makes for a summery, fruity treat! You can top this with fresh strawberries and whipped cream for a simple shortcake-like dessert, or drizzle with chocolate sauce to mimic the flavor of a chocolate-dipped strawberry.

4 tablespoons self-rising flour

4 tablespoons sugar

2 tablespoons beaten egg or liquid egg substitute

3 tablespoons milk

2 tablespoons vegetable oil

1/2 teaspoon vanilla extract

2 tablespoons seedless strawberry jam

Mix the flour and sugar in a mug. Add the egg, milk, oil, and vanilla and stir until well combined. Swirl in the strawberry jam. Microwave on high for 1 minute or until the top is just dry.

"The rule is, jam to-morrow and jam yesterday, but never jam to-day."
—Lewis Carroll, *Through the Looking-Glass*

Banana

This cake tastes like fresh, warm banana bread, but takes a lot less time! It's a great way to use up overripe bananas—just freeze your ripe, peeled bananas in individual ziplock bags, and you will have them on hand for when you want to mix up this easy cake.

4 tablespoons self-rising flour

4 tablespoons brown sugar

2 tablespoons beaten egg or liquid egg substitute

3 tablespoons milk

2 tablespoons vegetable oil

1/2 ripe banana, mashed

2 tablespoons chopped walnuts or miniature chocolate chips (optional)

Mix the flour and sugar in a mug. Add the egg, milk, oil, and banana and stir until well combined. Fold in the nuts or chips, if using. Microwave on high for 1 1/2 minutes or until the top is just dry.

Carrot Cake

You will not believe that this carrot cake takes 2 minutes to make. It tastes like a traditional carrot cake, but without all the time, mess, and stress! It is important to make sure the carrot is grated as finely as possible, so it can soften properly in the microwave. I use the medium holes on a box grater. Smear the finished cake with some cream cheese frosting, and voilà—spicy, delicious carrot cake in a flash!

4 tablespoons self-rising flour

4 tablespoons sugar

1/8 teaspoon cinnamon

1/8 teaspoon nutmeg

2 tablespoons beaten egg or liquid egg substitute

3 tablespoons milk

2 tablespoons vegetable oil

3 tablespoons grated carrot

2 tablespoons chopped walnuts or almonds

cream cheese frosting (page 24)

Mix the flour, sugar, cinnamon, and nutmeg in a mug. Add the egg, milk, oil, and grated carrot and stir until well combined. Fold in the nuts. Microwave on high for 1 minute or until the top is just dry.

Lime Coconut

A tropical breeze in a mug, this cake is full of sweet coconut and zesty lime flavor. It's great served with some sliced mango or fresh pineapple, and makes a refreshing, not-too-sweet treat perfect for summertime.

4 tablespoons self-rising flour

3 tablespoons sugar

1/4 teaspoon lime zest

2 tablespoons shredded sweetened coconut

2 tablespoons beaten egg or liquid egg substitute

3 tablespoons milk

2 tablespoons vegetable oil

Mix the flour, sugar, lime zest, and coconut in a mug. Add the egg, milk, and oil and stir until well combined. Microwave on high for 1 minute or until the top is just dry.

Apple Cinnamon

A warm, comforting cake that is perfect for fall, but made easy with applesauce! You can keep all the ingredients on hand and whip this up anytime your apple craving hits. The applesauce takes the place of the egg and some of the milk in this recipe. If you want to make the cake vegan, you can add another tablespoon of applesauce and leave out the milk entirely.

4 tablespoons self-rising flour

4 tablespoons brown sugar

1/4 teaspoon cinnamon

3 tablespoons applesauce

2 tablespoons milk

2 tablespoons vegetable oil

Cinnamon sugar, for topping

Mix the flour, sugar, and cinnamon in a mug. Add the applesauce, milk, and oil and stir until well combined. Sprinkle the top with cinnamon sugar. Microwave on high for 1 minute or until the top is just dry.

"I hate people who are not serious about meals. It is so shallow of them."
—Oscar Wilde, *The Importance of Being Earnest*

Pumpkin Spice

Oh, pumpkin, you seductive autumn temptress! Who doesn't love the comforting taste of pumpkin spice? These days, you can find pumpkin everything, but my favorite way to enjoy it is in a cake, especially this easy mug cake. Redolent with warm spices and that crave-worthy pumpkin flavor, this treat is well worth the 2 minutes it takes to make.

4 tablespoons self-rising flour

4 tablespoons brown sugar

1/4 teaspoon cinnamon

Pinch of ground cloves

1/8 teaspoon allspice

2 tablespoons canned pumpkin puree

3 tablespoons milk

2 tablespoons vegetable oil

1/2 teaspoon vanilla extract

Mix the flour, sugar, cinnamon, cloves, and allspice in a mug. Add the pumpkin, milk, oil, and vanilla and stir until well combined. Microwave on high for 1 minute or until the top is just dry.

Orange and Cream

This tastes like a Creamsicle in a mug. Sweet orange and rich vanilla combine to create a comforting yet refreshing cake that is perfect topped with fresh raspberries or drizzled with white chocolate. It is worth the extra step to squeeze fresh orange juice for this (and you already have the orange in your hand for zesting)!

- 4 tablespoons self-rising flour
- 4 tablespoons sugar
- 1/4 teaspoon orange zest
- 2 tablespoons beaten egg or liquid egg substitute
- 2 tablespoons orange juice
- 2 tablespoons vegetable oil
- 1/2 teaspoon vanilla extract

Mix the flour, sugar, and orange zest in a mug. Add the egg, orange juice, oil, and vanilla and stir until well combined. Microwave on high for 1 minute or until the top is just dry.

"A good cook is like a sorceress who dispenses happiness."

—Elsa Schiaparelli

Cranberry Almond

A sophisticated and unexpected indulgence, this cake is a snap to put together, thanks to canned cranberry sauce. This recipe uses the whole-berry variety, but you can use the smooth kind if you want. Almond extract gives it an extra boost of almond flavor, which goes really well with the cranberry, but feel free to substitute vanilla if you prefer.

4 tablespoons self-rising flour

4 tablespoons sugar

2 tablespoons beaten egg or liquid egg substitute

3 tablespoons milk

2 tablespoons vegetable oil

2 tablespoons whole-berry cranberry sauce, plus more for topping

1/8 teaspoon almond extract

2 tablespoons sliced almonds

Mix the flour and sugar in a mug. Add the egg, milk, oil, cranberry sauce, and almond extract and stir until well combined. Sprinkle the sliced almonds on top. Microwave on high for 1 minute or until the top is just dry. Top with some cranberry sauce.

Peach

This cake is for the peach cobbler lovers. The recipe uses canned peaches for simplicity and convenience, but if they are in season you can certainly use fresh, peeled, diced peaches. If peach Melba is your thing, swirl in some fresh or frozen (thawed) raspberries along with the peaches, or spread raspberry jam on top of the finished cake.

4 tablespoons self-rising flour

4 tablespoons sugar

2 tablespoons beaten egg or liquid egg substitute

3 tablespoons milk

2 tablespoons vegetable oil

1/4 teaspoon vanilla extract

1/4 cup diced peaches

White chocolate chips (optional)

Mix the flour and sugar in a mug. Add the egg, milk, oil, and vanilla and stir until well combined. Fold in the peaches. Microwave on high for 1 minute or until the top is just dry. Sprinkle on some white chocolate chips, if desired.

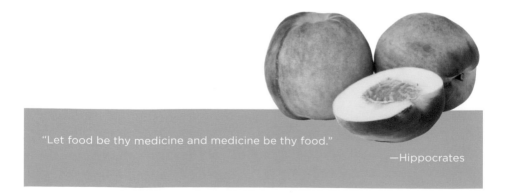

"Let food be thy medicine and medicine be thy food."

—Hippocrates

Lemon Soufflé

This bright, sunny cake is simplicity itself, and absolutely irresistible adorned with fresh berries and a sifting of powdered sugar. Freshly squeezed lemon juice is essential to the flavor of the finished cake, so don't substitute the bottled stuff, or you will lose out on the true lemon flavor that really shines in this recipe.

4 tablespoons self-rising flour

4 tablespoons sugar

1/4 teaspoon lemon zest

2 tablespoons beaten egg or liquid egg substitute

2 tablespoons milk

1 tablespoon lemon juice

2 tablespoons vegetable oil

Mix the flour, sugar, and lemon zest in a mug. Add the egg, milk, lemon juice, and oil and stir until well combined. Microwave on high for 1 minute or until the top is just dry.

CHAPTER FOUR

BOOZY BITES

Chocolate Stout

May the road rise up to meet you, and may your mug cake have the delicious flavor of a Guinness. The rich flavor of Irish stout is a perfect complement to this dark chocolate treat. You only need a few tablespoons, so you will be able to finish off the beer while enjoying your warm, comforting mug cake.

4 tablespoons self-rising flour

4 tablespoons sugar

3 tablespoons cocoa powder

2 tablespoons beaten egg or liquid egg substitute

3 tablespoons stout (like Guinness)

2 tablespoons vegetable oil

1/2 teaspoon vanilla extract

Mix the flour, sugar, and cocoa powder in a mug. Add the egg, stout, oil, and vanilla and stir until well combined. Microwave on high for 1 minute or until the top is just dry.

"I cook with wine. Sometimes I even add it to the food."

—W. C. Fields

Kahlúa Fudge

An espresso-based cake that features a decadent swirl of fudge and the boozy bite of Kahlúa, this is like a Mudslide in cake form! It tastes great topped with crushed cookies, but it's even better with whipped cream and a drizzle of Kahlúa for a nightcap.

4 tablespoons self-rising flour

4 tablespoons sugar

1 teaspoon instant espresso powder

2 tablespoons beaten egg or liquid egg substitute

3 tablespoons Kahlúa

2 tablespoons vegetable oil

1/2 teaspoon vanilla extract

2 tablespoons fudge sauce

Mix the flour, sugar, and espresso powder in a mug. Add the egg, Kahlúa, oil, and vanilla and stir until well combined. Swirl in the fudge sauce. Microwave on high for 1 minute or until the top is just dry.

"An empty stomach is not a good political advisor."   —Albert Einstein

Bourbon Butterscotch

Bourbon and butterscotch are a match made in heaven. This recipe was inspired by an old bourbon ice cream recipe from Food & Wine, *except this mug cake is a whole lot easier to make. It is perfect for when a bourbon-butterscotch craving hits but you just don't have the time or energy for homemade ice cream.*

4 tablespoons self-rising flour

4 tablespoons dark brown sugar

¼ teaspoon nutmeg

2 tablespoons beaten egg or liquid egg substitute

1 tablespoon bourbon

2 tablespoons milk

2 tablespoons melted unsalted butter

1/2 teaspoon vanilla extract

Butterscotch sauce for topping, if desired

Mix the flour, sugar, and nutmeg in a mug. Add the egg, bourbon, milk, butter, and vanilla and stir until well combined. Microwave on high for 1 minute or until the top is just dry.

Banana Whiskey

Whiskey brings a layer of boozy glory to a rich banana cake. The brown sugar lends a slight butterscotch flavor; if you want it more pronounced, swirl some butterscotch sauce into the batter before microwaving. Top with butter pecan ice cream and you have a sensational and comforting treat!

4 tablespoons self-rising flour

4 tablespoons brown sugar

2 tablespoons beaten egg or liquid egg substitute

1 tablespoon whiskey

2 tablespoons milk

2 tablespoons vegetable oil

1/2 ripe banana, mashed

Mix the flour and brown sugar in a mug. Add the egg, whiskey, milk, oil, and banana and stir until well combined. Microwave on high for 1 1/2 minutes or until the top is just dry.

"The gentle art of gastronomy is a friendly one. It hurdles the language barrier, makes friends among civilized people, and warms the heart."
—Samuel V. Chamberlain

Buttered Rum

The butter and brown sugar in this combine to create a rich butterscotch flavor that pairs beautifully with the dark rum. Be sure to use unsalted butter, since the self-rising flour has salt in it already. For extra rum flavor, use rum extract in place of vanilla.

4 tablespoons self-rising flour

4 tablespoons dark brown sugar

Pinch of ground nutmeg

2 tablespoons beaten egg or liquid egg substitute

1 tablespoon dark rum

2 tablespoons milk

2 tablespoons melted unsalted butter

1/2 teaspoon vanilla or rum extract

Mix the flour, sugar, and nutmeg in a mug. Add the egg, rum, milk, butter, and vanilla and stir until well combined. Microwave on high for 1 minute or until the top is just dry.

Tequila Lime

A margarita in a mug! This zippy little cake is a festive way to end a Mexican meal, and a great way to get more tequila into your diet. It is delicious with a scoop of sorbet, or some sliced mango or strawberries on top to kick up the tropical flavor.

4 tablespoons self-rising flour

4 tablespoons sugar

1 teaspoon lime zest

2 tablespoons beaten egg or liquid egg substitute

1 tablespoon tequila

2 tablespoons milk

2 tablespoons vegetable oil

Mix the flour, sugar, and lime zest in a mug. Add the egg, tequila, milk, and oil and stir until well combined. Microwave on high for 1 minute or until the top is just dry.

Baileys Irish Cream

Ahhh, whiskey and cream: What could be better? How about a whiskey-and-cream-flavored mug cake? This simple vanilla cake is a great way to use up the last of a bottle of Baileys, or to serve with Irish coffee at a dinner party. The cake itself is plain so as to let the whiskey flavor shine, but feel free to drizzle some sauce on it or top it with fresh berries.

4 tablespoons self-rising flour

4 tablespoons sugar

2 tablespoons beaten egg or liquid egg substitute

3 tablespoons Baileys Irish Cream

2 tablespoons vegetable oil

1/2 teaspoon vanilla extract

Mix the flour and sugar in a mug. Add the egg, Baileys, oil, and vanilla and stir until well combined. Microwave on high for 1 minute or until the top is just dry.

Eggnog

This little cake is a great way to use up leftover eggnog at holiday time, or to please the eggnog lovers in your life all year round. Just freeze some leftover eggnog in an ice cube tray, and pop out a cube when you have the urge to make a mug cake! Try sprinkling it with a dash of nutmeg before popping it into the microwave.

4 tablespoons self-rising flour

3 tablespoons sugar

2 tablespoons beaten egg or liquid egg substitute

1 tablespoon bourbon or rum

2 tablespoons eggnog

2 tablespoons vegetable oil

1/2 teaspoon vanilla extract

Mix the flour and sugar in a mug. Add the egg, liquor, eggnog, oil, and vanilla and stir until well combined. Microwave on high for 1 minute or until the top is just dry.

"Promises and pie-crust are made to be broken."

—Jonathan Swift

Chocolate
Grand Marnier

Chocolate and orange are a classic dessert combination, and for good reason. This elegant cake can be modified to suit your taste—if you want to amplify the orange flavor, add some freshly grated orange zest to the dry ingredients. Like more chocolate? Stir some chocolate chips into the batter before microwaving, or drizzle the cake with chocolate sauce.

4 tablespoons self-rising flour

4 tablespoons sugar

3 tablespoons cocoa powder

2 tablespoons beaten egg or liquid egg substitute

1 tablespoon Grand Marnier

2 tablespoons milk

2 tablespoons vegetable oil

Mix the flour, sugar, and cocoa powder in a mug. Add the egg, Grand Marnier, milk, and oil and stir until well combined. Microwave on high for 1 minute or until the top is just dry.

Rum Truffle

This cake pays homage to the delicious, old-time candy store rum balls, except it's a lot less time consuming to make! Using dark rum will add a more complex flavor, but you can use whatever you have, and it will be delicious.

4 tablespoons self-rising flour

4 tablespoons sugar

3 tablespoons cocoa powder

2 tablespoons beaten egg or liquid egg substitute

1 tablespoon dark rum

2 tablespoons milk

2 tablespoons vegetable oil

1/2 teaspoon vanilla extract

Mix the flour, sugar, and cocoa powder in a mug. Add the egg, rum, milk, oil, and vanilla and stir until well combined. Microwave on high for 1 minute or until the top is just dry.

CHAPTER FIVE

BEYOND CAKES

Oatmeal

An easy, healthy breakfast on the go can be yours in less than 5 minutes! You can customize this many different ways—try stirring in peanut butter or chocolate-hazelnut spread, or swap maple syrup for the honey. For a fruitier version, add applesauce or berries. You can leave out the egg if you want, but I like the little extra protein it adds and the firmer texture it gives the finished oatmeal.

1/2 cup quick-cooking oats

2 tablespoons beaten egg or liquid egg substitute

1/2 cup milk

1/3 banana, mashed

1/4 teaspoon cinnamon

2 teaspoons honey

Mix all the ingredients together in a mug. Microwave on high for 2 minutes.

Cheesecake

This simple recipe makes an adorable single-serving cheesecake perfect for times when you're craving it, but don't want to make a whole huge cake that takes an hour in the oven. It's a tiny bit more complicated than a regular mug cake, but it still comes together in less than 10 minutes from start to finish—the hardest part is waiting for it to chill! Then again, what's wrong with warm cheesecake?

CRUST

2 graham crackers, crushed into crumbs in a ziplock bag

1 teaspoon sugar

1 tablespoon unsalted butter, melted

CAKE

4 tablespoons cream cheese

2 tablespoons sour cream or plain Greek yogurt

2 1/2 tablespoons sugar

1 egg

1/2 teaspoon vanilla extract

Mix the graham cracker crumbs, sugar, and melted butter together. Press the mixture into the bottom of a mug. Whisk the cake ingredients together until you have a smooth batter, then pour on top of the crust in the mug. Microwave on high for 2 1/2 minutes. If the cake isn't set in the center, microwave in additional 15-second bursts until it's just cooked but not dry. You can cool and chill the cake in the mug, or invert it onto a plate for a more cake-like presentation. Either way, cool the cake until it is just warm, then cover and refrigerate until cold, about 2 hours.

Chocolate Chip Cookie

Craving a chocolate chip cookie, but don't want to make a whole batch? This easy recipe makes one big cookie in less than 5 minutes! Using a flat ramekin for this rather than a mug makes it more cookie-like, but you can achieve the same result in a regular mug. It's up to you.

1 tablespoon unsalted butter, melted

1 tablespoon sugar

1 tablespoon dark brown sugar

1/4 teaspoon vanilla extract

Pinch of salt

1 egg yolk

4 tablespoons flour

3 tablespoons chocolate chips

Mix all the ingredients in a mug until well combined. Microwave on high for 1 minute, or until the cookie is almost set but not completely (it will continue to cook as it cools).

Peanut Butter Cookie

It is important not to overcook this cookie to preserve the soft, chewy texture. It will continue to cook after you take it out of the microwave, so stop cooking it when the top is set but the cookie still looks soft in the middle. Be sure to use regular flour, not self-rising flour, so you don't end up with a cake instead!

3 tablespoons flour (not self-rising, or the cookie will be puffy and cakey)

Pinch of salt

2 tablespoons dark brown sugar

1 egg yolk

1 tablespoon butter, melted

1 tablespoon peanut butter (I like chunky, but creamy works, too)

1/8 teaspoon vanilla extract

Mix the flour, salt, and brown sugar in a mug. Stir in the egg yolk, butter, peanut butter, and vanilla and mix until well combined. Microwave for 45 seconds or until the top is set but the cookie is still soft in the middle.

Sugar Cookie

This easy recipe creates a classic, soft sugar cookie that is irresistible when topped with crunchy coarse sugar. This cookie makes a perfect snack or late-night treat, and you can top it with a scoop of ice cream for a modern interpretation of an ice cream sandwich.

3 tablespoons flour (not self-rising, or the cookie will be puffy and cakey)

2 tablespoons sugar

Pinch of salt

1 egg yolk

1 tablespoon butter, melted

1/4 teaspoon vanilla extract

Colored or coarse sugar, for sprinkling

Mix the flour, sugar, and salt in a mug. Add the egg yolk, butter, and vanilla and stir until well combined. Sprinkle with colored or coarse sugar. Microwave for 45 seconds or until the top is set but the cookie is still soft in the middle.

Chocolate Pudding

Classic homemade pudding is made by whisking milk, sugar, cornstarch, and cocoa powder over low heat until it is bubbling. When you make the speedy microwave version, it's hard to dissolve the dry ingredients completely, since you can't whisk during cooking. And that can result in lumpy pudding. To solve that problem, heat the milk before you add it to the dry ingredients, which helps them dissolve. Just microwave the milk in a glass measuring cup for a couple of minutes, until it is steaming hot but not boiling.

1 tablespoon cornstarch

2 tablespoons cocoa powder

3 tablespoons sugar

3/4 cup hot milk

1/4 teaspoon vanilla extract

Whisk the dry ingredients together, then pour in the hot milk in a steady stream, whisking constantly, until the dry ingredients dissolve. Stir in vanilla. Microwave on high for 1 minute or until it's boiling. Let the pudding cool, then chill in the refrigerator until cold, about 1 hour.

Berry Cobbler

You will be amazed by how easy it is to make a delicious, fruity cobbler for one in just minutes. This is a great way to take maximum advantage of fresh berry season, but you can also use frozen berries—simply add a minute or so to the cooking time. Be careful not to fill the mug more than two-thirds full, or it will boil over.

3/4 cup berries (blueberries, raspberries, strawberries, or a mixture)

5 tablespoons sugar, divided

1/3 cup self-rising flour

2 tablespoons unsalted butter, melted

2 tablespoons milk

1/4 teaspoon vanilla extract

Combine the berries and 4 tablespoons of the sugar in a mug and stir. In a separate bowl, mix the remaining tablespoon of sugar with the flour, butter, milk, and vanilla until a batter forms. Pour the batter on top of the berries. Microwave on high for 1 1/2 to 2 minutes or until the topping is set and the fruit is bubbling.

Apple Pie

This isn't a classic two-crust pie, but considering it takes only 5 minutes, it's a pretty good facsimile! If you want, you can use shortbread, vanilla wafers, gingersnaps, or other cookies for the crust. Just put them in a ziplock bag and crush them with a mallet or the bottom of a heavy glass until you have coarse crumbs.

2 graham crackers, crushed into crumbs

1 tablespoon butter, melted

1 small apple, cored, peeled, and diced

1 tablespoon all-purpose flour

1 tablespoon sugar

1/2 teaspoon apple pie spice

1 teaspoon freshly squeezed lemon juice

Mix the graham cracker crumbs and melted butter in a mug and press into the bottom to form a crust. In a bowl, mix together the apple, flour, sugar, apple pie spice, and lemon juice. Pour the apple mixture on top of the crust in the mug. Microwave on high for 2 minutes or until the apple is soft.

"A boy doesn't have to go to war to be a hero; he can say he doesn't like pie when he sees there isn't enough to go around."

—E. W. Howe

French Toast

This recipe just changed breakfast at your house. Now that you know the secret, you can have hot, delicious French toast whenever you want, in a couple of minutes. No skillet to wash or messy dipping process, just sweet, vanilla-scented French toast in a mug! Plain white sandwich bread works well, but you can use whole wheat or whatever you like. For special occasions, try challah or a croissant for an extra-rich treat.

2 slices bread (white works best, but you can use what you have), cubed

1 egg

4 tablespoons milk

1/8 teaspoon vanilla extract

Dash of cinnamon

Maple syrup, for pouring

Put the bread cubes in a mug. Whisk the egg, milk, vanilla, and cinnamon in a bowl. Pour the egg mixture over the bread, pressing it down a bit to make sure the bread can soak up the liquid. Microwave on high for 1 to 1 1/2 minutes or until the French toast is set. Drizzle with maple syrup.

Blueberry Muffin

An easy and tasty breakfast for one that will make it easy to forgo the expensive, calorie-laden muffins at the coffee shop! You can swap out the blueberries for raspberries, strawberries, or blackberries—or try a mix of berries for a burst of summer flavor.

4 tablespoons self-rising flour

4 tablespoons sugar

3 tablespoons milk

2 tablespoons butter, melted

1/8 teaspoon vanilla extract

2 tablespoons blueberries (fresh or frozen)

Sugar, for sprinkling

Mix the flour and sugar in a mug. Add the milk, butter, and vanilla and stir until well combined. Fold in the blueberries. Sprinkle sugar on top. Microwave on high for 1 minute if you're using fresh berries, and 1 1/2 to 2 minutes with frozen berries, or until the top is just set.

BONUS!

DUMP CAKE RECIPES FROM

BEST
DUMP
CAKES
EVER

AVAILABLE EVERYWHERE BOOKS ARE SOLD!

Apple Caramel Pecan

This decadent cake is a sweet, sticky caramel fantasy come true! The crunch of pecans adds textural contrast, and the drizzle of caramel sauce on top heightens the delicious butterscotch flavor. If you can't find caramel cake mix, substitute vanilla.

2 (21-ounce) cans apple pie filling

1 box caramel cake mix

1/2 cup butter, sliced into 12 thin slices

1/2 cup chopped pecans

1/2 cup caramel sauce

Preheat the oven to 350 degrees F. Grease a 9 × 13-inch pan. Spread the pie filling on the bottom of the pan. Sprinkle the cake mix over the pie filling. Place the butter slices evenly on top and sprinkle the pecans over the butter. Drizzle the caramel sauce on top. Bake for 35 to 40 minutes or until the cake is golden and the fruit is bubbling.

"One of the very nicest things about life is the way we must regularly stop whatever it is we are doing and devote our attention to eating."

—Luciano Pavarotti

Peach Gingerbread

Peaches and ginger are one of the world's best flavor combinations, and this cake showcases it to high glory. With just three ingredients, you can create an impressive dessert that is perfect all year round.

2 (21-ounce) cans peach pie filling

1 box gingerbread cake mix

1/2 cup butter, sliced into 12 thin slices

Preheat the oven to 350 degrees F. Grease a 9 × 13-inch pan. Spread the pie filling on the bottom of the pan. Sprinkle the cake mix on top of the fruit. Evenly place the butter slices on top. Bake for 35 to 40 minutes or until the cake is golden and the fruit is bubbling.

INDEX